THE
Star
A JOURNEY TO CHRISTMAS

DEVOTIONS THROUGH THE SEASON OF ADVENT
ON HOPE, LOVE, JOY, AND PEACE

OUTREACH®

The Star: A Journey to Christmas
© 2017 by Outreach, Inc.

Published by Outreach, Inc., Colorado Springs, CO 80919
www.Outreach.com

Unless otherwise noted, Scripture quotations in this publication are taken from THE HOLY BIBLE, NEW INTERNATIONAL VERSION®, NIV® Copyright © 1973, 1978, 1984, 2011 by Biblica, Inc.® Used by permission. All rights reserved worldwide. Also used is The ESV® Bible (The Holy Bible, English Standard Version®). ESV® Permanent Text Edition® (2016). Copyright © 2001 by Crossway, a publishing ministry of Good News Publishers. All rights reserved; and the King James Version.

ISBN: 9781635105612
Cover Design by Tim Downs
Interior Design by Alexia Garaventa
Written by Jeremy Jones

Printed in the United States of America

CONTENTS

INTRODUCTION

More than two thousand years ago, a star burst through the darkness and signaled the long-awaited but still unexpected birth of a Savior. Today another star shines, piercing the darkness of our lives with hope, love, joy, and peace. His name is Jesus and His light shines, drawing us into the journey of following Him.

This Advent season, you are invited to follow the star on a journey to Christmas. It's not just about the destination but about a journey of discovery that leads us toward hope, love, joy, and peace as we draw near to Jesus Christ, the light of the world.

Advent is a season that is officially observed in many churches. The four weeks before Christmas are set aside as a time of expectant waiting and preparation for the celebration of Jesus's birth. The term *advent* is a version of the Latin word that means "coming." But Advent is not just an extension of Christmas; it is a season that links the past, present, and future. Advent offers us the opportunity to share in the ancient longing for the coming of the Messiah, to celebrate His birth, and to be alert for His second coming.

There are some differences in the way people celebrate Advent. While the core concept is the same, some of the traditions and practices vary. This book is based on common practices, and we invite you to adapt it to match the traditions of your own church. One of the main traditions of Advent is the lighting of the candles on an Advent wreath. A circular evergreen wreath represents God's unending love for us. And the lighting of five candles throughout the season represents Jesus's coming to a world lost in darkness. Isaiah 9:2 says, "The people walking in darkness have seen a great light; on those living in the land of deep darkness a light has dawned."

This book contains devotions for each of the four weeks before Christmas. Based around the weekly Advent themes of hope, love, joy, and peace, there are seven devotions for each theme. There is also a devotion for Christmas Eve and one for Christmas Day. In addition, each of the sections contains an introduction page with a song to sing, verses to memorize, a question to ponder, and a verse to focus on throughout the week. We encourage you to use these sections as a guide for a weekly lighting of your own Advent wreath. Whether you do this alone, as a family, with friends, or as a small group, taking the time to practice the tradition of the lighting of the candles will add to the richness of your Advent experience. And singing the songs can make the experience especially fun and meaningful if you have kids. You'll also find a final section called "A Celebration of Christmas" filled with fun, creative ideas and activities to start some new family traditions or enhance your own celebration of Jesus's birth.

In a season often marked by frenzied busyness, Advent is an opportunity to set aside time to prepare our hearts. The tradition and the devotions in this book are designed to help us place our focus on a far greater story than our own—the story of God's redeeming love for our world.

So no matter what the department stores try to tell you, Christmas has not yet arrived. There is value as well as excitement in patient and expectant waiting. May this be a season of wonder for you. Just as the star led the Magi to Jesus so many years ago, may the Holy Spirit lead you as you embark on a journey of hope, love, joy, and peace.

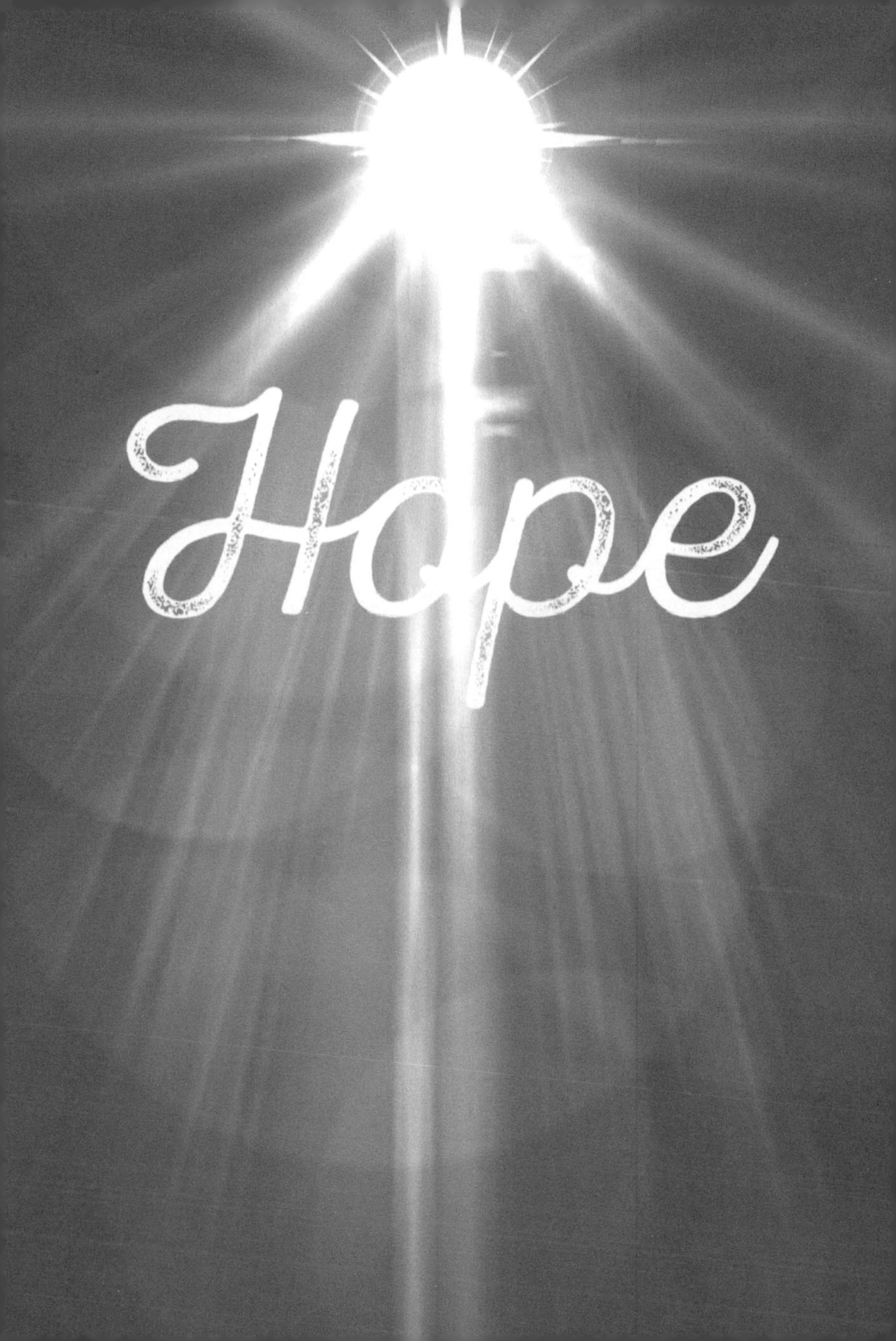
Hope

THE STAR LEADS TO HOPE

The first Sunday of Advent signifies the hope people felt in their hearts for a Savior to lead them out of dark and hard times. As we begin this season of Advent, we will spend the next seven days on a journey, following the star as it leads us to hope. In addition to the daily devotions, take time this week to light the first candle in your Advent wreath. (See Introduction for instructions.) Remember the prophecies that were fulfilled in Jesus's coming, express your desires for this season, and place your hope in the light of the world who was born as a baby in Bethlehem and who is coming again.

SING:

"Away in a Manger"

TELL:

"Therefore the Lord himself will give you a sign: The virgin will conceive and give birth to a son, and will call him Immanuel." —Isaiah 7:14

"Therefore, since we have been justified through faith, we have peace with God through our Lord Jesus Christ, through whom we have gained access by faith into this grace in which we now stand. And we boast in the hope of the glory of God." —Romans 5:1–2

ANSWER:

What do you hope for this season?

REMEMBER:

"May the God of hope fill you with all joy and peace as you trust in him, so that you may over-flow with hope by the power of the Holy Spirit." —Romans 15:13

1

HOPE'S LONG JOURNEY

I wait for the LORD, my whole being waits,
and in his word I put my hope.
—Psalm 130:5

In an age when drone delivery is a reality and information is constantly at our fingertips, we've become accustomed to immediate gratification. We get impatient with slow Internet connections and microwave ovens. So the idea of a long wait or a lengthy journey doesn't hold much appeal on the surface. But perhaps it is the journey, the process of the long wait, that is exactly what we need. We need time to recognize the depth of our need and to allow hope to build in our hearts. We need space to block out the many distractions of our lives. We need to quiet ourselves in the darkness so that we won't miss the arrival of the light of the world.

We need to wait and watch for the miracle of the birth of Jesus—when the God of the universe entered our world in order to transform us through His love.

Advent is just that—a long period of waiting, expecting, and looking forward to the coming of Jesus. In a rushed world, Advent is a deep breath that allows us to pause and then take each purposeful step on the journey as we follow the star toward Bethlehem. So we begin this season of waiting with hope in our hearts. Maybe your sense of hope is only the faintest glimmer right now or a mere spark. It's okay. Allow the long wait to be a place where hope grows—where it can build with each passing day and create space in your heart to receive the light of the world.

How do you feel about the idea of a long wait?

What choices can you make to carve out the time and space needed to engage the journey toward Christmas this Advent season?

Who can you invite to join you?

2

HOPE SHINES IN THE DARKNESS

The people living in darkness have seen a
great light; on those living in the land of the shadow
of death a light has dawned.

—Matthew 4:16

We typically think that light helps us see better, but sometimes we need the darkness in order to better see the light. When it comes to seeing the night sky, light is actually pollution. *National Geographic* reports that while about 2,500 individual stars are usually visible to the naked eye in the night sky, we can only see about 200 to 300 in a typical city today. Our city lights get in the way of us seeing the light of the stars. We have to go where it is dark to get a clearer vision of the light.

Hope works the same way. Only when we face the true darkness of our world, and of our own hearts, can we see the light of hope clearly. Jesus was born into a dark world full of hatred and fear. That same hatred and fear are present in countries, cities, churches, and families today. But our hope lies in the fact that God showed up unexpectedly in the midst of the darkest night. He shone His light into the world through a baby, and He invites us into that light.

Do you feel like you are living in darkness? Do the news headlines make you feel like you are living in the land of the shadow of death? Holiday glitz can artificially light our lives, but stepping into and facing the darkness allow us to see the true light of Christmas. Darkness can feel all consuming, but the darker it is, the brighter the smallest light seems to shine. Even in your deepest darkness, the light of hope shines, revealing the love of God, who is the source of all light.

What causes you to feel overwhelmed with darkness?

What in your life might be causing spiritual light pollution and keeping you from seeing the light of Jesus?

How will you step toward the light?

3

OUR ONLY HOPE

Be strong and take heart,
all you who hope in the LORD.

—Psalm 31:24

"Help me, Obi-Wan Kenobi. You're my only hope." Remember these epic words spoken by Princess Leia via a hologram message in *Star Wars*? In the midst of a hopeless situation, the princess of the Rebellion sends a desperate message. As she is about to be captured by the ruler of darkness, Darth Vader, she places a plea inside R2-D2, not knowing whether it will ever be seen or heard.

Do you ever feel like you've sent out your last desperate plea and now you wait and wonder if help will ever come? The good news of Advent is that help is on the way. Jesus is our only hope. There is nothing or no one else in this world that can win against the powers of evil and darkness—but Jesus is coming. To a world bound by sin and suffering, God sent His Son as a Savior. By God's perfect design, He showed up in Bethlehem as the fulfillment of the hope for a Messiah, and He will come again to complete the work He began, redeeming the world to Himself, setting everything right, and turning hope into reality once and for all. For now, in this Advent season, we can take heart and draw strength from the knowledge that our only hope has heard our plea and is coming to rescue and redeem us.

Have you reached the point in life where you realize God is your only hope?

What does it look like to cry out to Him and then to be strong and take heart?

4

HOPE DOES NOT DISAPPOINT

Not only so, but we also glory in our
sufferings, because we know that suffering produces
perseverance; perseverance, character;
and character, hope. And hope does not put us to shame,
because God's love has been poured
out into our hearts through the Holy Spirit, who has
been given to us.

—Romans 5:3–5

Do you ever wonder about those marriage proposals that get a "no" as an answer? Talk about disappointment! And probably an unexpected outcome. Or maybe you've been cut from a team, been fired from a job, or had a house contract fall through at the eleventh hour. You can fill in any number of your own examples. We've all felt the surprise and embarrassment of a situation where the result wasn't anything like what we'd expected or hoped for. Unfortunately, that's the way things often go in our broken world.

It's all the more reason we can rest and rely on the hope of Christ. His hope won't put us to shame. It's rooted in our eternally reliable God who won't fail us or forsake us. He has promised to fulfill His work of restoration in our lives and in our world. Even in our difficulties and suffering, He is able to transform our struggles into perseverance, growth, and hope that draw us ever nearer to Himself. Jesus's birth was the fulfillment of great hope. It also staked a beacon of hope within eternity for the completion of His return and ultimate work. As we purposefully wait and anticipate through the Advent season, we can also meet God in our struggles and allow Him to transform us through them. His hope will not disappoint us. He will not fail us.

Is there a situation or area of life where you find it difficult to hope?

How can you step out with confident hope in God's faithfulness?

5

THE ANCHOR OF HOPE

We have this hope as an anchor for the soul,
firm and secure.

—Hebrews 6:19

It's midnight, and the clear skies have turned dark and menacing. Your small boat that gently rocked you to sleep is now pitching and diving, thrown back and forth by surging swells and towering waves. The gentle breeze has turned into gale-force winds. Torrents of rain lash your craft, threatening to leave it battered and broken. Aboard that boat, you hope desperately for rescue. You hope for a sudden and miraculous change in the weather. You might even hope for a quick way out of the boat and onto dry land. In the metaphoric storms of our own lives, there is often no rescue, no miraculous change in situation, no quick escape—and that's where true hope comes in.

Hebrews tells us hope is an anchor for our souls—firm and secure. Hope doesn't remove the storm or remove us from the storm, but it holds us secure in the midst of it. It keeps us tethered and stable as the world pitches and boils around us. Hope is our anchor because we know the One who controls the storm. The same Child whose birth was announced by angels and marked by the light of a new star later demonstrated that He controlled the wind and the waves. And Jesus is more powerful than any storm we face in the world or within ourselves. He is our anchor, and He is secure. So we place our hope in Him and hold fast while the wind and rain and waves pound.

What is the storm in your life right now?

Are you anchored and holding fast, or are you being tossed by the waves of life?

What does it look like to allow hope to be your anchor?

6

UNRESOLVED HOPE

But if we hope for what we do not yet have,
we wait for it patiently.

—Romans 8:25

Do you ever listen to classical music? Odds are better that you listen more to the popular music of our times—those short, quick, often repetitive songs that fit into three-minute ditties just perfect for radio play. On the other end of the sound spectrum lies classical music. Classical music makes us wait in the ebb and flow of ever-building notes and movements and then finally provides resolution. It has an amazing way of creating desire as it builds and builds. Sometimes it contrasts its own melody, creating dissonance that causes us to long for and even expect resolution. The song or symphony would feel incomplete, unfinished, and even disturbing if that resolution never came. And yet there is beauty in the whole song, not just the resolution, so we listen and wait patiently and let our emotions ride the notes until the music reaches its end.

Waiting for Christ's coming at Christmas, as well as living in the waiting for His second coming, can feel like listening to a classical symphony. We hope for what we don't yet have, but we wait patiently for it. We can enjoy even the dissonance, letting our emotions swell with hope and desire and uncertainty and promise, knowing and trusting that the end will be even more beautiful because of the expectation built throughout.

What is your life's soundtrack in this season?

What promise can you cling to today that resolution is coming?

7

ACTIVE HOPE

Rejoice in hope, be patient in tribulation,
be constant in prayer.
—Romans 12:12 (ESV)

You know that old saying "A watched pot never boils"? It's not exactly true. Science proves that simply watching a pot actually does not change the speed with which water gets to the boiling point. But experience proves that watching can definitely change how long the process *feels*. Doing nothing but watching can make even a short wait feel like an eternity, tempting us to give up or give in to distractions. And while the waiting work of hope is good for our hearts and minds, even Advent can feel intolerably long if we don't put hope into action.

How? Paul told us in Romans to rejoice in hope. Laugh. Tell stories with friends. Listen to music. Enjoy good food. Worship God. Be present to the people in your life and patient with the challenges and hardships you face. Paul also told us to be constant in prayer. No matter what your season of waiting on hope looks like, talk to God about it. Listen for His voice. Spend time in prayer, seeking the wisdom and peace of God. And choose to rejoice, no matter how dark the night seems. Because as you do these things, you put hope into action—and that commitment helps to create and sustain an active hope that does not grow weary and does not give up.

What can you do to transform your waiting into an active hope?

How can you rejoice in hope today?

What does it look like to be constant in prayer?

What are you praying for today?

Love

THE STAR LEADS TO LOVE

The second Sunday of Advent signifies love and reminds us that Jesus was sent to us because of God's great love for us. Follow the star as it leads you on a journey to love over the next seven days. Along with the daily devotions, take time this week to light the second candle in your Advent wreath. Let the reality that God's love came crashing into our world permeate your life this week. Experience the depth of His love and allow that love to overflow to others.

SING:
"Hark the Herald Angels Sing"

TELL:
"'The days are coming,' declares the LORD, 'when I will fulfill the good promise I made to the people of Israel and Judah.'" —Jeremiah 33:14

"For I am convinced that neither death nor life, neither angels nor demons, neither the present nor the future, nor any powers, neither height nor depth, nor anything else in all creation, will be able to separate us from the love of God that is in Christ Jesus our Lord." —Romans 8:38–39

ANSWER:
When do you feel most loved by others? By God?

REMEMBER:
"And I pray that you, being rooted and established in love, may have power, together with all the Lord's holy people, to grasp how wide and long and high and deep is the love of Christ, and to know this love that surpasses knowledge—that you may be filled to the measure of all the fullness of God." —Ephesians 3:17–19

8

LOVE, LIGHT, AND LIFE

For God so loved the world that he gave his one and only Son, that whoever believes in him shall not perish but have eternal life.

—John 3:16

The love of a parent for a child is often upheld as the strongest love of all. It is natural for parents to love their child more than anything, to be willing to sacrifice and even die for their child. It's true of the animal world as well as humans. This is the reason a mama bear with cubs is much more dangerous than a female bear alone. There is an instinct for love and protection deep within parents for their child. So it's really hard for us to imagine the amazing love God has for our world that motivated Him to give His only Son to be born and die for us.

But that is exactly the love we celebrate this Advent season—a love so great that God broke through space and time in order to send His own Son into the world. And with that love came light and life. When the Christ child we celebrate in Advent and Christmas had grown up and was teaching His disciples, He said, "I am the light of the world. Whoever follows me will never walk in darkness, but will have the light of life" (John 8:12). As we celebrate the unfathomable love of God this Advent, we also celebrate the inextinguishable light and eternally fulfilling life that Jesus offers to each one of us.

Do you find it easy or difficult to accept the amazing love God has for you?

How has your relationship with your own parents impacted the way you see the love of God?

How can you lean into the love, light, and life that Jesus brings this season?

9

THE GIFT OF LOVE

Every good and perfect gift is from above, coming down from the Father of the heavenly lights, who does not change like shifting shadows.

—James 1:17

If there is anyone who is famous for changing like the shifting shadows, it's the Grinch. Yes, that strange green Dr. Seuss character who returns every Christmas season with his sneaky attempts to steal Christmas from the poor Whos down in Who-ville. Dressed up as Santa Claus, he pretends to deliver gifts when really he is stuffing them back up the chimney, doing his very best to take away everything that represents the spirit of Christmas.

So what does the Grinch have to do with Advent? He's the stealer of gifts—the exact opposite of the giver of all good gifts, who sent the perfect gift in the birth of Jesus. The baby born in a stable was the ultimate gift of love, given from the heart of our steadfast, unchanging Heavenly Father. Rather than trying to trick us into something or take the things that bring us joy, He is the source of true, unconditional love. In the midst of a world that is constantly changing and shifting under our feet, in the midst of hurt and distrust created by people in our lives who have broken promises, God offers us the perfect gift of love: the unexpected arrival of a baby who changes our world and our hearts for eternity. Even the Grinch's transformation pales in comparison.

When have you most felt the magnitude of the gift of love sent in Jesus?

How do you feel knowing that God has given you such a good and perfect gift?

What steps can you take to focus on love during this Advent season?

10

FIRST LOVE

This is how God showed his love among us: He sent his
one and only Son into the world that
we might live through him. This is love: not that we
loved God, but that he loved us and
sent his Son as an atoning sacrifice for our sins.

—1 John 4:9–10

We often think of love as a feeling or maybe an action.
Either way, we think of it as something we feel or do,
something that comes from somewhere deep inside us,
something that strikes us with powerful emotion or
maybe something we can create more of if we just try
hard enough. But this Advent season, love is a reminder
that it's really not about us. It's not about what we feel or
think or do. It's about what God has already done.

Advent is about anticipating and remembering that
before we could have even imagined loving God, He
loved us and sent His Son into the world for us. Love
started with God. There is great freedom in that truth

because it means we don't have to try harder; we don't have to get our act together before we can celebrate Christmas. Whether you are feeling close to God or distant from Him right now, it doesn't change the fact that God loved you first, regardless of what you think, feel, or do. No matter where you are on your spiritual journey with God, let's celebrate Him in this Advent season as the source of all love. And let us pause to receive and savor the love always flowing from Him into our hearts and lives.

Are there any ways that this season creates pressure on you to feel more love for God?

How does remembering God loved you first change your perspective?

11

NO FEAR IN LOVE

There is no fear in love.
But perfect love drives out fear.

—*1 John 4:18*

If someone told you Christmas was a holiday of fear, you would probably think they were crazy. It's all about lights and presents and love and peace and joy, right? But looking closely at the Christmas story as recorded in the Bible reveals that there sure were a lot of people who were afraid. Mary and Joseph were both afraid of the uncertain, if not miraculous, circumstances they found themselves in. The angel had to tell the shepherds not to be afraid. King Herod was so afraid he ordered that babies be killed. We can even assume the wise men might have felt some fear since they went home by a different route instead of returning to Herod. That's a lot of fear for a story that is supposed to be full of peace and joy.

But that is the real world Jesus entered—our world. He didn't come to a world free of fear; He came to drive out fear with love. Think of a glass full of muddy water. As clear water is poured into the glass, it eventually displaces the dirty water until only clear water remains. The same is true with love. Perfect love drives out fear; it overwhelms and replaces anxiety, fright, or dread. As you follow the star toward Christmas, don't worry if your heart is full of fear. God knows the realities of our world, and He knows your deepest fears. But as you walk toward Christmas, be willing to open your heart and let God's love pour in, washing through you until fear is displaced by pure love.

What fears do you face right now?

Do you believe God's perfect love can drive out fear?

How can you open your heart to His love this Advent season?

12

DEEP LOVE

And I pray that you, being rooted and established in love,
may have power, together with all the Lord's
holy people, to grasp how wide and long and high and
deep is the love of Christ, and to know this
love that surpasses knowledge—that you may be filled to
the measure of all the fullness of God.
—Ephesians 3:17–19

The Mariana Trench is the deepest part of the world's oceans. If Mount Everest were to be dropped into the trench at its deepest point, the summit would still be a mile underwater! And while scientists have studied it, including two manned trips to the ocean floor of the trench, much remains unknown. It's hard to imagine an area so deep beneath the surface of the ocean's waves. Even when we hear the scientific measurements, it's hard to grasp that kind of depth.

God's love sometimes feels a bit like the Mariana Trench—a love so deep it is almost unfathomable. We can study it, we can learn about it, but there is no end to the experience of it. In Paul's letter to the Ephesians he called it a "love that surpasses knowledge." And yet God invites us into the depths of His love. Instead of overwhelming the world with the depth and power of His love, He chose to make that deep love approachable by sending His Son as an infant, born in a stable, vulnerable and fully human. Jesus experienced life in our world as fully and deeply as possible. As a result, we are invited to dive deep and experience the power of God's love beyond measure.

Do you ever feel overwhelmed by the depth of God's love?

What helps you experience in a personal way His love that surpasses knowledge?

How can you open your heart to Jesus, who brings all the fullness of God's love into our world?

13

WIDE LOVE

The true light that gives light to everyone was coming into the world. He was in the world, and though the world was made through him, the world did not recognize him. He came to that which was his own, but his own did not receive him. Yet to all who did receive him, to those who believed in his name, he gave the right to become children of God.

—John 1:9–12

Have you ever stopped to think about the crazy cast of characters God chose to witness the coming of Jesus? A carpenter, a teenage unwed mother, some shepherds, wise stargazers from a far-off country. If we were to write the perfect Christmas story, we might have chosen some more respectable people. But this collection of people is a perfect picture of what God intended to do through Jesus: to shine the light on everyone and to cast the net of His love so wide into the world that it brings in people from the edges.

The Gospel of John says Jesus came to His own but His own didn't recognize or receive Him, so He opened the offer of salvation to anyone who believes. He threw wide the doors of love and invited everyone in! The amazing thing about our journey to Bethlehem is that it is open to everyone. *Everyone.* No matter how ragtag our hearts or lives may feel, you and I and all of us are welcome. We are all invited to celebrate the fact that Jesus's love broke down all the barriers and draws us to personally experience the love of God.

Where are you on your journey toward Christmas?

Do you feel in the center of God's love or on the edge, hoping His love extends wide enough to pull you in?

Is there anyone in your life who needs to be invited into the wide love of Jesus?

14

LOVE NEVER FAILS

Love is patient, love is kind. It does not envy, it does not boast, it is not proud. It does not dishonor others, it is not self-seeking, it is not easily angered, it keeps no record of wrongs. Love does not delight in evil but rejoices with the truth. It always protects, always trusts, always hopes, always perseveres. Love never fails.
—1 Corinthians 13:4–8

Who do you find it hardest to love? Some might say the command to love our enemies is the hardest. Others might argue that loving those closest to us is the most difficult. Either way, in 1 Corinthians 13 Paul gave us a long list of what love is to look like. The standard can feel overwhelming until we realize that this isn't just a command, it's a description of the gift God has given us in Jesus. God's love sent in Jesus promises to be all these things for us, to us, and in us.

As we continue our journey toward Christmas, we can celebrate the amazing qualities of the love God has given: patience, kindness, humility, forgiveness, protection, trust, hope, and perseverance. Most importantly, we celebrate that God's love never fails. Even in the darkest moments before Jesus was born, love was present and at work. And in the darkest hours of our own lives, love has not failed us. God is present and His love is at work in and around us, even when we can't see it. No one expected love to show up in a stable in Bethlehem. Keep your eyes open for love to show up in the places you least expect.

Do you feel encouraged or discouraged by Paul's description of love in 1 Corinthians 13?

Do you trust that God's love never fails?

How can you take time to watch for and be open to love showing up in unexpected ways this Advent season?

Joy

THE STAR LEADS TO JOY

The third Sunday of Advent signifies joy and reminds us of the angel's good news told to the shepherds. Follow the star as it takes you on a journey to joy over the next seven days. Along with the daily devotions, take time this week to light the third candle in your Advent wreath. Imagine yourself on the hillside where the joyous news was announced by heavenly hosts. As you watch for joy in the world around you during this season, surrender the pain and fear of your life and ask God to fill you with the gift of His joy.

SING:

"Joy to the World"

TELL:

"An angel of the Lord appeared to them, and the glory of the Lord shone around them, and they were terrified. But the angel said to them, 'Do not be afraid. I bring you good news that will cause great joy for all the people.'" —Luke 2:9–10

"Let the heavens rejoice, let the earth be glad; let the sea resound, and all that is in it. Let the fields be jubilant, and everything in them; let all the trees of the forest sing for joy. Let all creation rejoice before the LORD, for he comes." — Psalm 96:11–13

ANSWER:

How do you imagine it might have felt to be a shepherd that first Christmas?

REMEMBER:

"Though you have not seen him, you love him; and even though you do not see him now, you believe in him and are filled with an inexpressible and glorious joy." —1 Peter 1:8

15

JOY FOR THE JOURNEY

Consider it pure joy, my brothers and sisters, whenever
you face trials of many kinds, because you know
that the testing of your faith produces perseverance.
Let perseverance finish its work so that you
may be mature and complete, not lacking anything.

—James 1:2–4

If you were alive in the 1980s, the phrase "No pain, no gain" may bring to mind '80s-style aerobics workouts. That was the era when the phrase gained popularity, largely thanks to Jane Fonda in her workout videos, but the concept that great accomplishment requires hardship and sacrifice is an ancient one. None of us wishes for hardship, but the apostle James said to count trials as joy for this very reason—perseverance leads to maturity and completeness.

This isn't a mind-set of denial, forcing us to stuff the pain and pretend to be happy. Instead, it is a mind-set of looking beyond the immediate circumstances to the growth it can bring in our lives. We often think the presence of trials strips us of joy, but when we turn that perspective around, it helps us to see the hope for a better resolution turns into the joy of growth and strength. If you find yourself on a journey full of trials right now, don't allow it to strip your joy. Instead, choose to let hardship increase your reliance on God and allow it to bring greater joy as you journey toward completeness with Him.

What is your attitude about your current trials?

Do you find them strengthening you or stripping you of joy?

How can you reset your perspective toward one of growth and joy even on life's difficult journey?

16

TEARS AND JOY

Those who sow with tears will
reap with songs of joy.

—Psalm 126:5

Take a good look at some of the things gardeners plant, and you just might be horrified. Roots, tubers, rhizomes, and bulbs aren't exactly pretty to look at. In fact, looking at them above ground, you might say they are the exact opposite of beauty. Common sense would tell you to throw them away because they have no use. But these ugly clumps planted in the soil grow into some of a garden's most colorful and vibrant flowers. What goes into the ground is unrecognizable when it emerges a few seasons later.

The same is often true of tears. They are painful and seem contradictory to joy. Common sense tells us they have no worth except to bring us down as a product of our sadness. But the psalmist said they can grow into something beautiful: "Those who sow with tears will reap with songs of joy" (Psalm 126:5). They can bring us a cathartic cleansing in the moment, watering the fruit of healing for the future.

If you find yourself in a season of reaping with songs of joy, then sing out and share your joy encouragingly with others. If you are in a season of sowing with tears, draw close to those around you and take comfort—a season is coming that will be filled with songs of joy. The Good Gardener whom we await in Advent will cultivate vibrant good and beauty even out of our pain and difficulty.

What season do you find yourself in?

How can looking forward to a healing harvest help you with the tears of today?

What song of joy will you begin to sing today?

17

CHOOSE JOY

The LORD has done it this very day;
let us rejoice today and be glad.
—*Psalm 118:24*

Advent is a time of waiting, but it is not a time of in-action. Advent involves action! It's an active waiting, considering the things the Lord has done and antici-pating the coming of the Savior of the world. The jour-ney toward joy at Christmas is not something we sit around and wait for; while it is a gift from God, it is also something we get up and do. Rejoicing is an action we choose, not just a feeling that comes our way or happens to us. Break down the word, and we discover re-joy. It signifies the act and process of choosing to celebrate and exclaim a sense of thankfulness and joy.

But where do we find the motivation? Knowing that God has already accomplished His purpose of sending redeeming love into the world gives us reason to re-joice no matter what other circumstances surround us.

Choosing joy doesn't have to involve a dance party (although it might!), but it does involve purposeful thankfulness and deep appreciation for the work God has done and is doing in our lives and in our world through His Son, Jesus. Choosing to be thankful for even the simplest things and continually resetting our focus on thankfulness will profoundly impact our sense of joy.

What are you thankful for today? List three things that are reasons to rejoice. If you find it difficult, start small but sincere: the heartbeat inside your chest, the smile of a stranger, the feel of wind on your face.

How can you choose joy and celebrate those things God has done today?

18

JOY
AND WORSHIP

When they saw the star, they were overjoyed.
On coming to the house, they saw the child
with his mother Mary, and they bowed down and
worshiped him.

—*Matthew 2:10–11*

The Magi set out on a life-changing journey to follow the brightest star they'd ever seen. Did they fully understand its meaning? We're not sure, but they knew they couldn't ignore it. Have you ever set out on a journey because you felt led by God? Have you ever felt drawn by something that you couldn't completely explain but couldn't ignore? It can be exciting, scary, exhausting, exhilarating, and so many other things along the way. But what happens at the end of a life-changing journey? When the mission you set out on is finally accomplished?

In the story of the Magi, they saw the star that came to rest over the place where Jesus was, and they were overjoyed. Then they bowed down and worshiped Him. The end of following Jesus is always Jesus. The final result of a life-changing journey is worship. Yes, you will be transformed along the way, but that ultimate transformation comes in and through Jesus. This Advent season, as you journey toward Bethlehem, let joy and worship go hand in hand as you rejoice in the gift of Jesus and respond by worshiping Him.

Where are you on your journey of following God?

How can you prepare your heart for worship when you arrive at the end of the Advent journey?

19

MOTIVATED BY JOY

*And let us run with perseverance the race marked out
for us, fixing our eyes on Jesus, the pioneer and
perfecter of faith. For the joy set before him he endured
the cross, scorning its shame, and sat down at
the right hand of the throne of God.*

—Hebrews 12:1–2

Have you ever watched a retriever play fetch? With its
eyes fixed on the ball, it will go over, across, under, or
through *anything* to get to that round sphere of pure joy.
It can be comical to see just what those dogs will endure
simply for the joy of fetching a ball so they can bring
it back and do it again and again. We could all learn a
lesson from those dogs, a lesson of taking our eyes off
everything that consumes our lives and fixing them on
Jesus in order to run the race set out for us.

The Bible says Jesus Himself endured the greatest pain—suffering and death on the cross. Why? For the joy set before Him. He was motivated by the joy He knew rested on the other side at the right hand of His Father. As we go through life, that is where our focus should be—on the joy that we know is to come when we meet our Savior face-to-face. As we anticipate the joy of Jesus's arrival at Christmas, Advent also reminds us of the journey toward when He comes again and makes joy truly complete. There is joy throughout the journey, but even that will pale in comparison to what lies at the journey's end.

Do you find yourself motivated by fear or by joy?

What are you focused on?

How would the choices you make today look different if you shifted your focus to being motivated by joy?

20

JOY TO THE WORLD

But the angel said to them, "Do not be afraid.
I bring you good news that will cause great joy for all
the people."

—Luke 2:10

Organizations that install clean water pumps in villages throughout developing countries know the meaning of something that brings great joy for all the people. Photos of exuberant faces tell it all. Security, improved health, opportunity for education—even life and death—are all wrapped up in the stream of clear water that pours from a pump. And the beauty is that it is not just for the young, the old, or those with power but for all the people. Everyone in the village benefits from the water.

That was the message of the angel who appeared to the shepherds the night Jesus was born. This gift was not just for a few; it was good news of great joy for *all* people. And as the shepherds traveled to see the baby and then told others, they experienced the connection of joy. But the angel began its announcement by telling the shepherds not to fear. Fear isolates; joy is meant for all the people it connects. Despite all our differences, this Advent we are connected to the whole world by a message of joy that is meant for all people everywhere.

What do you see isolating you from the people around you?

How can you use the message of joy to create connection with others?

Who do you know who might feel left on the outside and could benefit from the connecting power of joy?

21

UNCONTAINABLE JOY

You will go out in joy and be led forth in peace;
the mountains and hills will burst into
song before you, and all the trees of the field
will clap their hands.

—Isaiah 55:12

Advent is not just a personal journey toward joy but a journey of all creation toward the redeeming work of God. The whole earth rejoices, proclaims His glory, and sings songs of joy. The Bible is filled with examples of the ways nature expresses the glory and joy of the Lord. Psalm 19:1 says, "The heavens declare the glory of God; the skies proclaim the work of his hands." Isaiah 55:12 tells of mountains and hills bursting into song and trees clapping their hands. These are pictures of uncontainable joy.

When we truly encounter the life-changing gift of Jesus, our reaction matches that of all creation. When we come face-to-face with the truth of God's endless love for us, shown through the birth of Jesus to save us all, the result is uncontainable joy that can spill out to everyone we meet in everything we do. When Jesus entered Jerusalem before His betrayal and crucifixion, the people rejoiced and sang songs of praise. Officials who didn't like the spectacle told Jesus to silence His followers. Instead, Jesus responded, "I tell you, if they keep quiet, the stones will cry out" (Luke 19:40). The message of God's love and the eternal life He offers can cause even lifeless stones to cry out in praise—now that is uncontainable joy! And even if we find our hearts cold and hard, Jesus can restore them to vibrant life.

What is the most uncontainable thing you can imagine (water, fire, love, etc.)?

How does the image of nature erupting in uncontainable joy impact your concept of the joy God gives?

When do you find yourself overflowing with joy?

Peace

THE STAR LEADS TO PEACE

The fourth Sunday of Advent signifies peace and reminds us that Jesus came to bring peace and goodwill. We will spend the next seven days during this final week of Advent following the star to peace. In addition to the daily devotions, take time this week to light the fourth candle in your Advent wreath. In a world that seems to be filled with more violence and chaos than peace, allow God to be your peace. Whatever circumstances you are facing, find rest this week in the peace of Christ.

SING:

"O Little Town of Bethlehem"

TELL:

"And suddenly there was with the angel a multitude of the heavenly host praising God, and saying, Glory to God in the highest, and on earth peace, good will toward men." —Luke 2:13–14 (KJV)

"Peace I leave with you; my peace I give you. I do not give to you as the world gives. Do not let your hearts be troubled and do not be afraid." —John 14:27

ANSWER:

In what area of your life do you feel the deepest need for God's peace?

REMEMBER:

"Now may the Lord of peace himself give you peace at all times and in every way. The Lord be with all of you." —2 Thessalonians 3:16

22

PEACE IS A PERSON

For to us a child is born, to us a son is given, and the government will be on his shoulders.
And he will be called Wonderful Counselor, Mighty God, Everlasting Father, Prince of Peace.

—Isaiah 9:6

Peace is most often defined as a state of quiet, rest, or calm. Or perhaps you think of peace as freedom from or the absence of war, violence, chaos, or noise. Peace is and can be all of those things. But on our journey toward Christmas, we discover that peace is actually much more than just an abstract state of being. Peace is a person.

Isaiah foretold the birth of a child who would be called the Prince of Peace, and that prophecy was fulfilled in the birth of Jesus. Throughout Jesus's life and teaching we see that peace comes from the person of

Jesus and the gift of the Holy Spirit—God's presence with us. By sending His Son, God sent peace into the world. And when we abide with Him, we abide with peace. One day, Jesus will restore the absence of war and violence to our world. Today, He will restore our hearts to rest, calm, acceptance, forgiveness, love, and all of the traits that spring forth from His identity.

When you seek peace, do you seek freedom from difficulty and chaos or do you seek Jesus?

How does recognizing peace as a person change the way you pursue peace?

How can you discover peace in God's presence this Christmas?

23

THE GIFT OF PEACE

Peace I leave with you; my peace I give you. I do not give to you as the world gives. Do not let your hearts be troubled and do not be afraid.

—John 14:27

Our world is much better at trading than giving. In fact, most gifts are given with the expectation of getting something in return. If you look around the world at nations struggling to find peace, there is often a lot of talk about peace deals. Both sides want peace, but neither side is willing to give it away freely. Peace deals are brokered as a compromise of priorities in the hope that everyone will be satisfied enough to stop fighting each other for a time. It's a pattern that can be seen between countries, political parties, siblings, spouses, and friends.

That is why when Jesus promised His disciples the gift of His peace, He assured them that He does not give as the world gives. His was not a trade agreement or a peace deal involving give-and-take. Jesus wanted His followers to receive and experience the peace that comes from the Holy Spirit. It was a free gift for them and remains a free gift for us today. And the nature of the gift allows us to experience true peace, without troubled hearts or fear. Jesus has offered a gift unlike anything the world gives, and we can rest in the true gift of His peace.

Does it feel strange to you to accept a free gift?

Do you feel you need to give something in return?

Do you live with a troubled heart or feel afraid?

How can you step into freedom from fear by receiving Jesus's gift of peace?

24

A SPIRIT OF PEACE

But the fruit of the Spirit is love, joy, peace,
forbearance, kindness, goodness, faithfulness,
gentleness and self-control.

—Galatians 5:22–23

Have you ever noticed that great artists often come from families of great artists? Teachers from families of great teachers? Musicians from families of great musicians? Athletes from families of great athletes? Some call them gifted with certain abilities. Sure, they must work to develop and nurture their skills, but there is a strong element of the natural gift received from their parents.

When we are one with Christ, the Holy Spirit lives in and through us, instilling in us the gifts or fruits of the Spirit. Yes, we have to work at nurturing these fruits in our lives, but their source is the Holy Spirit.

His traits are gifts given to us. Like love and joy, peace is a fruit of the Spirit. We can't create it on our own. We can take steps toward it, but ultimately we must accept peace as a gift from the Holy Spirit, who is the spirit of peace. The more closely we live in relationship with God, the more He develops those gifts within us. As we journey through Advent, we have the opportunity to purposefully invite the growth of the fruit of the Spirit in our hearts and minds and to accept the peace that He offers and instills.

What natural gift(s) have you received from your family?

How has living with your family fostered and grown that gift in your life?

How will you surround yourself with the Holy Spirit to allow Him to nurture and grow the fruit of peace in your life this week?

25

PEACE OF MIND

You will keep in perfect peace those whose minds are
steadfast, because they trust in you.

—Isaiah 26:3

On June 3, 2017, rock climber Alex Honnold made history when he scaled a nearly 3,000-foot granite wall in Yosemite National Park known as El Capitan without using any ropes or other safety gear. Free soloing, as it is called, is an incredibly dangerous form of climbing that requires not only physical strength and skill but an incredible mental strength to prepare and control the power of fear. People who know Honnold attribute his success on the rock to his tireless preparation and an amazing ability to keep his mind steadfastly focused in order to overcome the fear that he acknowledges he feels. That steadfast mind keeps him calm (not to mention alive!) during record-breaking climbs.

Most of us will never dream of a climb like Honnold's, but in the challenges of life, we too benefit from a steadfast mind. The Bible tells us that God keeps in perfect peace those whose minds are steadfast. The act of trusting God completely opens us to the peace that He provides. It is a practice that requires continual refocusing—the Advent season is a perfect time for intentionally doing so. But when we get rid of our spiritual safety nets and set our minds steadfastly on God's power to sustain us, we experience His perfect peace.

When have you experienced the deepest sense of God's peace in your life?

What distracts you from having a mind steadfastly focused on God?

What do you falsely rely on for spiritual safety instead of trusting God's power?

26
POWERFUL PEACE

I have told you these things, so that in me you may have peace. In this world you will have trouble. But take heart! I have overcome the world.

—John 16:33

"Peace, be still." With these simple words, Jesus calmed the wind and waves that frightened His disciples on the Sea of Galilee (see Mark 4:35–41). Faced with the reality and power of nature, even Jesus's closest friends were afraid. But Jesus quickly demonstrated that He is more powerful than anything in our world and His power is our peace. In John 16, Jesus didn't promise a life free of trouble. In fact, He told His disciples they would definitely face it. But He reminded them that their peace was secure in His power. He has overcome the world! Notice He didn't say He *would* overcome the world. He said, "I *have* overcome the world." The work is already done—we know the end of the story—so what do we have to fear?

Even as we wait and anticipate His second coming when all will be brought to completion, we know that through His birth, death, and resurrection He has already beaten sin and death. Therefore, when we face chaos, disorder, and discord in our world, we can find rest in the knowledge of His power, order, and peace. Whether your world is swirling with a tempest or the whirlwind of the holidays, take heart in this Advent season: Jesus, our coming King, has overcome our world and offers us His peace!

Do you think of peace as powerful?

How does Jesus's power bring you peace?

How can you remind yourself that you know the end of the story and have nothing to fear?

27

PRAYER AND PEACE

Do not be anxious about anything, but in every situation,
by prayer and petition, with thanksgiving,
present your requests to God. And the peace of God,
which transcends all understanding, will
guard your hearts and your minds in Christ Jesus.
—Philippians 4:6–7

The egg drop is a classic school science experiment. Each team gets an egg and can use all kinds of materials, from foam to Bubble Wrap to straws, to build a capsule that will protect the egg when it is dropped from a designated height. The teams can't change anything about the egg or remove the egg from the experiment, but they can get creative about how to guard the egg from the effects of the impact of the fall. When the contraptions are complete, they are dropped from the top of a stairwell or a building roof to see which eggs will survive impact and which ones crack. The eggs are still fragile, but many survive because they are safely surrounded.

Sometimes we can feel like the experimental egg—hoping not to break from the impact of life's challenges. The great news is that the Bible tells us exactly how to cushion the impact, how to guard our hearts and minds. Prayer allows us to hand over all our anxiety to God. It shifts our perspective to God and allows us to engage in dialogue with Him. In doing so, our hearts and minds are changed as they are surrounded and guarded with peace in Christ Jesus. Prayer provides an extra cushion of peace—that's way better than Bubble Wrap!

What do you feel anxious about this Advent season?

How can you make prayer a regular part of your journey to Christmas?

Make an effort to write down the ways you see prayer leading to the peace that guards your heart and mind.

28

THE BLESSING OF PEACE

May the God of hope fill you with all joy and peace
as you trust in him, so that you may overflow with hope
by the power of the Holy Spirit.
—Romans 15:13

It's hard to imagine a summer garden this time of year. But that barren patch of soil that sits covered in snow for now will be unrecognizable at harvesttime when it overflows with veggies galore. If you've never had your own garden, perhaps you've been the lucky recipient of another gardener's excess—say, an overflow of tomatoes or zucchini or peppers. Just as the overflow of garden produce can be shared generously with others, the overflow of God's good gifts in our lives is meant to be a blessing.

This Advent season, as you continue to journey toward Christmas, may the Holy Spirit fill you with all hope, love, joy, and peace. And as you gather with others at the manger to worship the King whose birth was announced by the light of the brightest star, may the overflow from your life be a blessing to others. May you experience the blessing given to the Israelites in Numbers 6:24–26: "The LORD bless you and keep you; the LORD make his face shine on you and be gracious to you; the LORD turn his face toward you and give you peace." And may you in turn pass it on to family and friends and others whose lives intersect with yours in this season and beyond.

Where do you find yourself this season—overflowing with hope, love, joy, and peace or in need of being blessed by the abundance of someone else?

How can you take time today to open your heart to the blessing of peace through the presence of the Holy Spirit in your life?

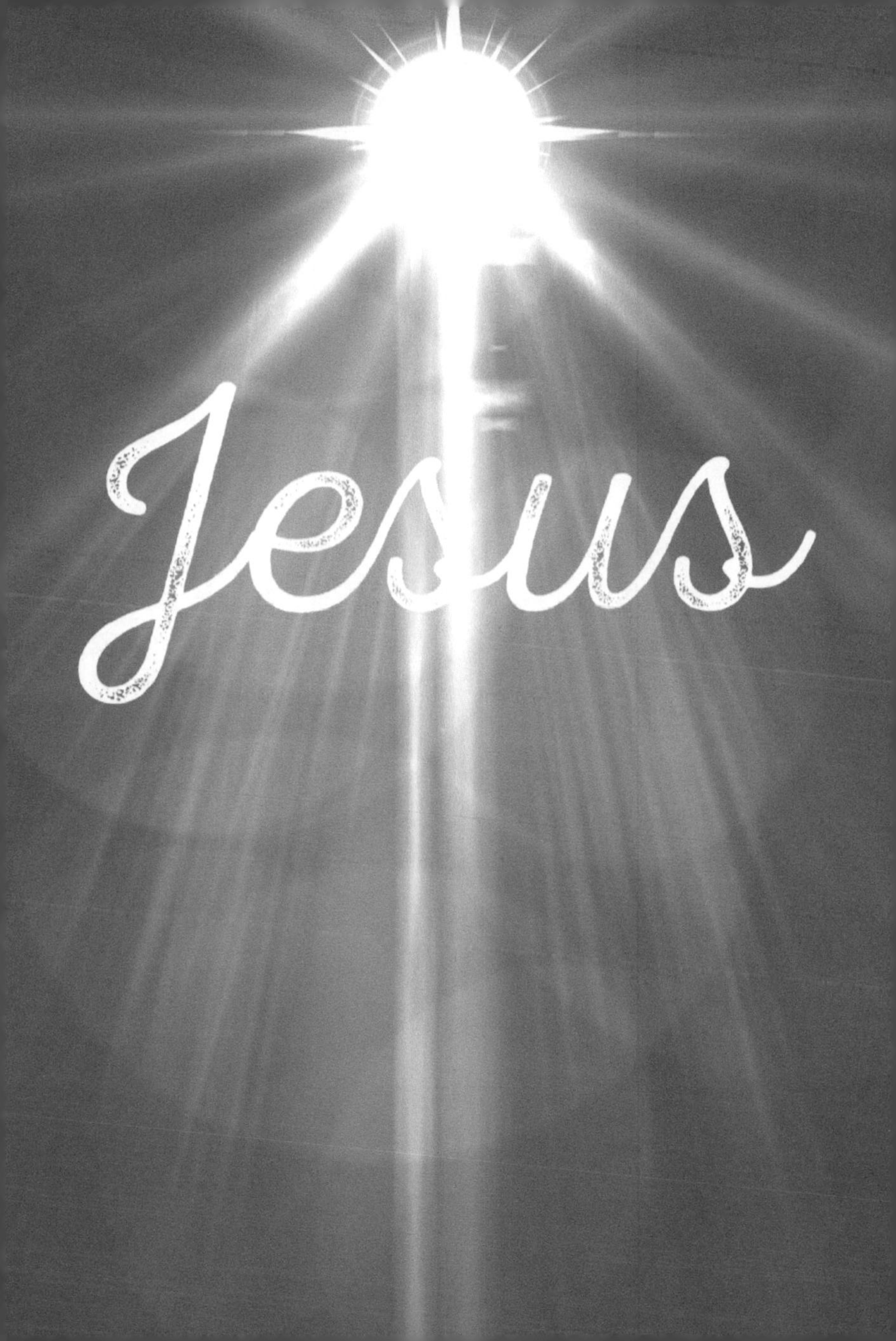
Jesus

THE STAR LEADS TO JESUS

The fifth and final candle of Advent represents Jesus Christ. This candle signifies the ultimate reason for our Christmas journey—the baby Jesus, God's only Son, the Savior of the world. Jesus is truly the reason the star of Christmas shone, and He is the source of all the things we've discovered on this Advent journey—hope, love, joy, and peace. Celebrate the birth of Jesus! The waiting is almost over; the Messiah is coming. And even as we celebrate His arrival in our world, our anticipation grows, and we continue to live with longing and expectation for His second coming when His work will be complete and all the world will be reconciled to Him. Yet even now on the eve and day of Christmas, we rejoice. Christ has come! He will come again!

SING:

"Silent Night" (as well as all the other carols from each of the weeks in Advent)

TELL:

"'She will give birth to a son, and you are to give him the name Jesus, because he will save his people from their sins.' All this took place to fulfill what the Lord had said through the prophet: 'The virgin will conceive and give birth to a son, and they will call him Immanuel' (which means 'God with us')." —Matthew 1:21–23

"Every good and perfect gift is from above, coming down from the Father of the heavenly lights, who does not change like shifting shadows." —James 1:17

ANSWER:

What is one of your favorite Christmas celebration memories?

REMEMBER:

"The Word became flesh and made his dwelling among us. We have seen his glory, the glory of the one and only Son, who came from the Father, full of grace and truth." —John 1:14

29

CHRISTMAS EVE:
THE STAR SHINES IN THE NIGHT

The heavens declare the glory of God; the skies proclaim the work of his hands.

—Psalm 19:1

Science is full of unsolved mysteries, and the Star of Bethlehem falls right in line. Throughout history, experts have not been able to agree on exactly what the star was—a supernova, a comet, a rare conjunction of planets? Others toss aside natural explanations and focus on the fact that God's miraculous presence with His people took many forms of light throughout the Bible. Moses saw a burning bush. The Israelites were led by a pillar of cloud by day and a pillar of fire by night. When Jesus appeared to Saul on the road to Damascus, Saul was blinded by a bright light. The mystery of whether the light in the night sky was a natural occurrence or a divine manifestation of God's presence or a combination of both remains, but all options are miraculous.

A star led the wise men to the new King. God's light still shines in our darkness through the Holy Spirit and guides us into the light of Jesus. While we can't explain it, the star is consistent with the psalmist's praise for the fact that the heavens declare God's glory. And so we celebrate the star that announces the arrival of—and shows the way to—hope, love, joy, and peace, present in our world through the Son of God. And our response, wherever we are on our journey with God, is to be the same as all those who encountered the light—follow and worship. No matter how dark your life is tonight, no matter where you find yourself, no matter what pain or sadness you feel, the star's light shines for you. It is God's invitation to come and adore the newborn King and to discover new life.

What keeps you from stepping into the light tonight?

Will you bow down and worship the newborn King?

30

CHRISTMAS DAY:
THE STAR LEADS ON

*Again Jesus spoke to them, saying, "I am the light
of the world. Whoever follows me will not walk in darkness, but will have the light of life."*

—John 8:12 (ESV)

Do you remember that amazing gift you opened as a kid? The one you couldn't wait to tear into and start playing with right away . . . only to discover your cool new power toy was missing something? Batteries not included! The most exciting thing under the tree got tossed aside because it had no power. How tragic it would be if a similar thing happened in our hearts—after traveling the journey of Advent and following the star toward Bethlehem, what if we found that it was the end? The light went out, the star faded, no power . . . batteries not included.

The good news is that Jesus *is* the power source. The star marked His arrival, but He is the light of the world! The journey continues as we continue to follow Jesus, who leads us and gives the light of life. The words to "We Three Kings" say, "O, star of wonder, star of night, star of royal beauty bright, westward leading, still proceeding, guide us to thy perfect light." This Advent the star has done just that—led us to "thy perfect light." And so we head out into the world with our way lit by Jesus, the true light of the world.

What are some ways you will continue the journey of Advent in the new year?

How will you allow the light of Jesus to shine through you?

A CELEBRATION OF CHRISTMAS

Each person's celebration on Christmas Eve and Christmas Day will look different depending on your place in life. You may be single, married, have kids or not, or wish you had kids or not. You may be celebrating new life or grieving the loss of a loved one. You may be caring for older parents, young children, or someone who is sick. You may have every moment of your Christmas Eve and Christmas Day already scheduled, or you may be wondering how in the world you are going to fill all the holiday hours. This section of ideas is not meant to simply provide you with more stuff to do. It's an invitation to fun and reflection and community. It's an invitation for you to step back and celebrate the baby born in Bethlehem—our Savior, the light of the world. You may already have plans and traditions, or you may be looking for ideas to start some. Use and adapt the ideas here to add creativity to your own celebration of Jesus's birth.

CREATE

Candle Star Jars

Collect one small glass jar per person (small jelly or canning jars work well—no lids needed). On the outside of the jars, have each person attach medium-size star stickers or cut out paper star shapes and glue on. Put a votive or tea light in the bottom of each jar. Use the jars as a centerpiece on the table or line them up along a bookshelf or mantle. Light the candles and watch for the star shadows they cast on a nearby wall. For a more involved project, place the star stickers on the jars and then spray-paint the outside of the jars red, green, gold, and silver. While the paint is still drying, remove the stickers. When you light a candle inside the jar, instead of a star shadow, your candle will create a glowing star on the nearby wall.

Folding Stars

Gather all kinds of household items such as recycled magazines, colored paper, string, straws, Popsicle sticks, pipe cleaners, etc. Then search online for simple instructions on how to make stars with your supplies.

There are so many options out there! Choose based on age and ability and then have fun creating unique stars.

Garland of Light

Cut out stars (or save time and buy some cutouts from a local dollar store or teacher supply store). Give each person in the family one star for each of the other members of the family. (If you have five family members, each person gets four stars.) On each star, write one person's name and something about that person that makes them shine—a quality that makes them unique and special. Then hang the stars on a garland or banner where they can be seen and read by all.

Star Memories

Provide a pile of star cutouts and pens. Turn on some music and have friends or family members write down favorite memories from the past year—one memory per star. Place all the stars in a jar. Then on New Year's Eve, read through the stars together as a way to reflect on the good times of the past year.

PLAY

Star Word Wars

Write the following on note cards. Using a one-minute timer, the object is for one person on each team to try to get their team members to say the word at the top of the card. They can use other words, hand motions, etc., but they cannot say any of the words listed on the card. Add to the fun by creating cards with your own words!

Star: light, sky, twinkle
Ornament: hang, tree, decoration
Candle: light, burn, bright
Manger: sleep, baby, Jesus
Shepherd: sheep, angel, flock
Gift: present, open, give
Holly: deck, boughs, berry
Reindeer: Rudolph, sleigh, animal
Candy Cane: stripe, red, mint
Snowman: corncob pipe, balls, cold
Baby: born, child, little

Sing It

Keep older kids engaged in activities by adding this test of their Christmas song memory to any downtime. Play favorite Christmas songs, but press pause at random spots in each song. See who can sing the next line first!

Hang the Stars

For young kids, play a version of pin the tail on the donkey by blindfolding them and having them pin a star on the stable. For older kids, play a minute-to-win-it game. Place paper star cutouts on the ends of two tables. Each team has one minute to blow (using just breath, no hands) as many stars as possible off the other end of the table.

Follow the Star

Set up a treasure hunt in advance by writing down a clue for finding the next clue location. Add to the fun by writing clues on star cutouts. Hide a clue at each location that points to where the next clue can be found. When the teams reach the final one, they should find a treasure—perhaps a coupon for free hot cocoa, Christmas Eve pajamas, or a Christmas movie to watch together.

Stargazing

If you have a clear night, get outside and look up at the stars. Download a phone app that allows you to see what stars you are looking at. Then think of all the songs you know about stars and sing them while you gaze at the night sky. If you have a local planetarium or telescope open to the public, plan to take a trip to learn more about the stars in the sky.

SHARE

Star Cookies

Bake star-shaped cookies together and decorate them. Then deliver packages of Christmas cookies to friends and neighbors. Or better yet, invite them over to share the cookies together.

Star Door Hangers

Cut out large stars from poster board and attach trailing ribbons or tinsel beneath one end of the star. Then write a verse and a personal note or Christmas wish on them. Deliver to friends and neighbors, or visit a local nursing home to brighten the holiday of those who may feel alone.

Caroling

If you live in a neighborhood, pull a group together to go caroling! Provide battery-powered candles, song lyric sheets, and even instruments. Then go door-to-door spreading Christmas cheer. If going door-to-door isn't an option, let the people come to you—gather on a street corner and sing for the people passing by.